So Cute! Baby Animals

Goats

By Julia Jaske

Baby goats like to eat.

Baby goats like to smile.

Baby goats like to sniff.

Baby goats like to drink.

Baby goats like to bleat.

Baby goats like to jump.

Baby goats like to run.

Baby goats like to explore.

Baby goats like to stand.

Baby goats like to climb.

Baby goats like to rest.

Baby goats like to play.

Word List

Baby	drink	stand
goats	bleat	climb
eat	jump	rest
smile	run	play
sniff	explore	

60 Words

Baby goats like to eat.
Baby goats like to smile.
Baby goats like to sniff.
Baby goats like to drink.
Baby goats like to bleat.
Baby goats like to jump.
Baby goats like to run.
Baby goats like to explore.
Baby goats like to stand.
Baby goats like to climb.
Baby goats like to rest.
Baby goats like to play.

Published in the United States of America by Cherry Lake Publishing Group
Ann Arbor, Michigan
www.cherrylakepublishing.com

Book Designer: Melinda Millward

Photo Credits: © imagevixen/Shutterstock, cover, 1; © Nick Barounis/Shutterstock, 2; © Photosite/Shutterstock, 3; © Linas T/Shutterstock, 4; © Ivan Lonan/Shutterstock, 5; © schubbel/Shutterstock, 6; © Slatan/Shutterstock, 7; © Jolanta Beinarovica/Shutterstock, 8; © CreativeFireStock/Shutterstock, 9; © schubbel/Shutterstock, 10; © Kerry Hargrove/Shutterstock, 11; © Liana Elise/Shutterstock, 12; © Rita_Kochmarjova/Shutterstock, 13; © cynoclub/Shutterstock, 14

Copyright © 2023 by Cherry Lake Publishing Group
All rights reserved. No part of this book may be reproduced or utilized in any form or by any means without written permission from the publisher.

Cherry Blossom Press is an imprint of Cherry Lake Publishing Group.

Library of Congress Cataloging-in-Publication Data

Names: Jaske, Julia, author.
Title: Goats / written by Julia Jaske.
Description: Ann Arbor, Michigan : Cherry Lake Publishing, [2022] | Series: So cute! Baby animals
Identifiers: LCCN 2022009897 | ISBN 9781668908822 (paperback) | ISBN 9781668912010 (ebook) | ISBN 9781668913604 (pdf)
Subjects: LCSH: Goats—Infancy—Juvenile literature.
Classification: LCC SF383.35 .J37 2022 | DDC 636.3/907—dc23/eng/20220330
LC record available at https://lccn.loc.gov/2022009897

Cherry Lake Publishing Group would like to acknowledge the work of the Partnership for 21st Century Learning, a Network of Battelle for Kids. Please visit http://www.battelleforkids.org/networks/p21 for more information.

Printed in the United States of America
Corporate Graphics